PRAISE FOR J. R. SOLONCHE

I0146902

"J. R. Solonche can pack so much humor and linguistic playfulness into such tight bundles, it feels like 1,000 clowns issuing from a VW Bug. He can also fit a lot of darkness and mortality into them, which feels more like 1,000 clowns dressed like Marilyn Manson issuing from a VW Bug. Solonche can be crass the way only the truthful can be, mischievous as a child with his hands in the honey jar, or even aphoristic and proverbial like a modern day Martial. Though you never know which Solonche you're going to encounter on the next page, he's a great bunch of guys to get to know."

   —STEPHEN CRAMER is winner of the Louise Bogan Award and the National Poetry Series.

"The poems of J. R. Solonche catch the reader off guard in playful profundity. While always mindful of the tradition of poetry masquerading as direct statement (the like of W. C. Williams, Robert Bly, Robert Creeley, and Charles Bukowski), J. R. Solonche nevertheless 'makes it new' through his masterful use of understatement, aphorism, word play, and anaphora—raising poem after thoughtful poem from the familiar and often overlooked 'little things' of the poet's day-to-day encounter with the world."

   —PHILLIP STERLING is author most recently of *And Then Snow.*

"Sample one by one these epigrammatic, epiphenomenal, Epicurean episodes as if they were puffs from a tower of pastry. Savor the zest of lemon, the pinch of sea salt, the dollop of crème fraiche, and the absence of any more sugar than necessary to ease the ingestion of truth. A feast for fanatics of language and lovers of pith. I'm not sure what pith is, but I know it when I see it."

—SARAH WHITE is author most recently of *Iridescent Guest*.

"Solonche, an accomplished poet, employs various forms in this compilation, including haiku, prose poem, and free verse. The poems often imaginatively enter into the natural or material world via anthropomorphic similes . . . Many works have an aphoristic quality that recall Zen koans, and they can be playfully amusing or even silly . . . A strong set of sympathetic but never sentimental observations."

—KIRKUS REVIEWS

"These short poems are an extraordinary amalgam of wit, close observation, humor, and clear-seeing. Each one singles out and illuminates an ordinary moment—ordinary, that is, until the poet explodes into a miniature epiphany. Easy of access and frequently profound, J. R. Solonche's poems induce in me a state of delighted surprise."

—CHASE TWICHELL is author of *Horses Where the Answers Should Have Been: New and Selected Poems*.

"In a style that favors brevity and pith, J. R. Solonche brings a richness of experience, observation, and wit into his poems. Here is the world! they exclaim. And here and here and here! Watched over by ancient lyric gods—Time, Death, and Desire—we find the quotidian here transformed."

—CHRISTOPHER NELSON is editor of *Green Linden Press.*

"The history of book blurbs is littered with high falutin' praise, whacky and wild metaphors, written to impress not to inform. All I need to say about J. R. Solonche's poems is that they are good, really, really good. So much so that they have a high 'I-wish-I'd-written-that' factor. That's a compliment I hand out to very few poets writing today. You want wit? You want humor? You want erudition? You want them all mixed into poems? Try Solonche. You won't be disappointed. Envious perhaps, but not disappointed."

—JOHN MURPHY is editor of *The Lake Contemporary Poetry Webzine.*

"The best feature of Solonche's poetry is its diversity. Everyone who encounters this volume (including the postman who delivers it to you) will find something in it to understand and remember—and a great deal to enjoy."

—TONY BEYER is author of *Anchor Stone,* finalist for the New Zealand Book Award.

THEN
MORNING

poems
J. R. Solonche

SHANTI ARTS PUBLISHING
BRUNSWICK, MAINE

THEN MORNING

Copyright © 2024 J. R. Solonche

All Rights Reserved

No part of this document may be reproduced or transmitted in any form or by any means without prior written permission of the publisher, except in the case of brief quotations embodied in critical reviews.

Published by Shanti Arts Publishing

Designed by Shanti Arts Designs

Shanti Arts LLC
193 Hillside Road
Brunswick, Maine 04011
shantiarts.com

Printed in the United States of America

ISBN: 978-1-962082-36-5

Library of Congress Control Number: 2024946894

TITLES BY THIS AUTHOR

CONTENTS

PART I

PART II

PART III

PART I

SEPTEMBER PASTORAL

All clouds have been exiled to a different sky.
A hawk shows a crow what a circle is.

The wind—What a polite breeze!—minds its manners.
The black cherry cuts its leaf losses.

The spider wort came out, came out, came out wherever it was.
Two white butterflies came out from the same place.

I want to welcome the overhead jet.
Some things, however, must remain unwelcome guests.

Tree frogs chirp in the trees.
Crickets chirp in the grass.

I know of no reason to know which is which.
Much of the best poetry is anonymous.

THE WIDE WAY

Do you ever dream about going home?
Do you ever dream about taking the long way home?
In dreams about the long way home, you never get home,
    do you?
Do you ever dream about taking the wide way home?
In dreams about the wide way home, you also never get
    home, do you?
But don't you get closer to home that way?
Don't you get so close you can see home that way?
Don't you get so close, so close, you are at the door of home?
Isn't the wide way home worse than the long way home?
O, isn't the wide way so much worse?

DARK BRIGHTNESS

Milton knew a bright
darkness. This September
afternoon half in shade,
half in sun, wholly in hell,
I know a dark brightness
around all, all around.

EVERY NIGHT, YES, EVERY NIGHT

Every night, yes, every night,
I ask forgiveness of the world for leaving it behind,
for saying it is not welcome to go with me into that other place,
that place of dreams where I could be alone,
as far as possible away from it,
but every night the world puts on its mask,
and lights its lamp and follows me there.

DELPHINIUM

Demanding beauty,
it held its breath
until it turned blue,
but is there now not
one god, just one,
to show it mercy
and let it breathe again?

THE LAKE IS A GOOD LISTENER

The lake is a good listener.
It listened to me today when I needed it most.

As I drove around it playing Ellington, it listened approvingly.
Its eyes sparkled in the sun.

Its smile was a mile wide.
Its laugh was ninety feet deep.

The great blue heron tapped its foot in its shallows.
O yes, today the lake listened approvingly to my despair.

YOUNGER

I drove around the lake.
I drove clockwise.

Then I drove counterclockwise.
Then I drove counterclockwise again.

I wanted to see if I was younger after driving
    counterclockwise twice.
I wasn't younger.

I was older.
I was twelve minutes older.

But the top was down.
And the music was Ellington.

And the Ellington was loud.
And the music was Basie.

And the Basie was loud.
And the top was down.

So I felt younger.
I felt thirty again.

But I don't remember being thirty.
So I felt being thirty for the first time.

I drove home.
I looked in on my wife.

She was still seventy-seven.
She still had Alzheimer's.

She was still in the hospital bed.
She was still asleep or awake.

I still couldn't tell the difference.
Nor still could she.

SNAKE

I saw a dead snake in the middle of the road.
"Oh, I am sorry someone did this to you," I said.
"Don't be. There is neither justice nor mercy in this world,"
said the snake. "There is only me in the middle of this road,
a road which was not here when my forebears divided the grass."

THE BEAUTIFUL GIRL

in the coffee shop
looked like so many
different actresses that
she looked like none.
Too bad. She will be
hard to remember.

AND THERE WAS A DREAM

And there was a dream,
And in the dream there was a hill,
And on the hill there was a tree,
And on the tree there were the words, *Only the sadness.*

OCTOBER PASTORAL

Five geese have lost their *vee*.
Or they have not practiced enough.

The deer have eaten two chrysanthemum plants.
They were the two farthest from the house.

The zebra grass covers half the stone wall.
Half is still visible through the weeds.

There hasn't been a hummingbird in days.
The yellow wasps have the feeder to themselves.

A fox bounds out of the woods.
It is in no particular hurry.

A vulture claims a dead squirrel on the road.
Like little brother crow, black becomes you beautifully.

TRYST

I want to have a tryst with you.
I want it to be the real thing,
the genuine article. I want it to
be under a clock or at the booth
at the back of a dark restaurant.
I don't want to be wearing a red
carnation. I want to be wearing
my one rumpled suit and my one
tie. I want to have five o'clock
shadow from not shaving that
morning. I want you to see me as
I am. I want you to see me as I will
be for the rest of our lives. And you,
you must come as you are.

THE STAIRS IN THE MANSION OF BILL BLASS

So
informally
elegant
(or is it
elegantly
informal?)
anyway
sleek
spare
slender
sexy
lithe &
black &
white &
sort of
what this
poem
would
look
like in
a short
black
dress

HAY BALES IN A FIELD

Because they are not like anything else,
these hay bales in this field
in this valley
at the end of October, I wish I were an artist,
a painter who scorns similes, who bad-mouths metaphors.
You know, one of those lucky son-of-a bitch, motherfucking bastards.

MY READER

Someone bought a copy
of my *Selected Poems*
2002–2021 at Good Books
in Cornwall, New York, and
I cannot help but wonder
who it was. I would like to
think it was a woman, well-
educated, perhaps with a
doctorate, not in literature,
but in biology or art history
or better yet, in psychology,
plain looking in her fifties,
glasses, divorced or widowed,
who went to the coffee shop
next door, opened the book at
random, smiled, and, for the first
time in her life, wrote a poem,
a poem about buying a book of
poetry, ten times better than this.

FOR ALL THE WORLD

"A poet looks at the world as a man
looks at a woman,"
says Wallace Stevens.
This is an easy one,
for the world, like a woman, is a mystery.

RUTH STONE'S HAIR

Her granddaughter couldn't think
of the name of her grandmother's
hairdo. "It's from the 1940s. Is it
the quiff?" "No, don't call it that.
Quiff means slut in British slang,"
I said to the screen while watching
the video about Ruth Stone. "It's a
pompadour," I said to Bianca as
though she could hear me down
the years between us. Did she never
write a poem about it, about her hair,
itself a poem standing and bowing over
her forehead like a great red peony?
"Never mind, Bianca. It was really
a Victory Wave, your grandmother's
wonderful wave of victory," I said
to the screen, waving goodbye.

NOVEMBER PASTORAL

Now is the tipping point.
Now there are more leaves on the ground than on the trees.

Now the trees cannot cover their nakedness.
Now they shiver in the wind.

Now the sun tests its strength against the weight of the shadows.
Now the shadows weigh down the afternoon.

Now the hawk has a better playing field.
Now the crow has a longer echo chamber.

Now the vulture has an abundant table.
Now the deer cannot outrun the gun.

Now the wind wins.
Now the wind sings its victory song into the endless ear
     of the night.

MRS. MINOGUE

You spoke of her often.
How, when your mother and father
were both at work, she minded you and
your sister in the Bronx apartment.
She was Irish and Catholic and told you
stories of bogeymen in closets and
stories of leprechauns under the bed
to frighten you. But then she laughed
because you were frightened.
She wanted to console you, so she
frightened you. She wanted that because
she didn't have children of her own.
She was Irish and Catholic and brought
you to church sometimes. Your sister hated
church. She hated the priests and the Latin.
The smell made her sick. The incense made
her dizzy and sick. But you liked it.
You liked the priests and the Latin.
You loved the smell of the incense.
You loved to watch the censer swing back
and forth. You loved to follow the smoke arc
back and forth. When you smile now,
are you thinking of Mrs. Minogue?
Are you remembering the arc of a smell?

STAR

Here is a star on this branch tending to its business.
It is the business of burning.

It is the business of making light.
Star, let me sit on this branch with you.

Star, I want you to teach me how to make light.
No, I do not need to learn how to burn.

You do not need to teach me that.
I already know how to burn.

I know all too well.
But star, star, I need to learn how to make light.

Let me sit on this branch with you, star.
Let me sit and learn how to make light.

SKY

Such a blue sky today!
Such a blue sky today,
it must have forgotten what clouds are.
Such a blue sky today,
this is how much it must be in love with the sun.

THE CHAIR

Has anyone ever told you how sharp your elbows are?
No? Let me be the first.
Just look at my arms, or what's left of them.
And the way you shake your right leg is annoying as hell.
I'm slumping to the right.
Maybe you should shake your left leg to even me out.
Or stop altogether.
At least you don't make me dizzy with incessant swiveling.
And you do wipe Rachel's hairs off after she sleeps on my lap.
All right, I confess.
We make a good couple, you and I.
Yes, you tall, gaunt, bony poet you, I'm comfortable with you.
Sit for as long as it takes.
Your poems are short, and they don't take long.
I'll support you.
I'll take your load off, off your mind, off your heart.

IRISH HANDCUFFS

I asked for Irish Handcuffs.
She never heard of it.
They almost never do.
Even in the Irish bars they almost never do.
I told her what it was.
A shot of Jameson in one hand, a Guinness in the other.
Does it matter which hand? she asked.
It may to some but not to me, I said.
Now that you know how to serve Irish Handcuffs, it won't matter.
Nobody will ever ask for one ever again, I said.
She was a college student.
I asked her what she was studying.
To become a funeral director, she said.
Want another one? she asked.
Not today, I said.
I still have two years to go, she said.
Okay. Good to know. I'll be back, I said.
And I'll know Irish Handcuffs, she said.
And I'll know who I want to embalm me, I said.
She laughed.
I didn't laugh.
But she had two years to go.
And a lot can happen in two years.

PART II

THIS MORNING CAME EARLY

This morning came early.
It had a lot on its mind.
It needed to unburden itself.
"This better be good," I said.
"O yes, it is. It is good," said the morning.
It stared at me in silence for what seemed like an eternity.
It was an eternity.
It was good.

THIS MORNING WAS DIRTY

This morning was dirty.
It wanted to be seen clearly.
"I want to be seen clearly," it said to me.
"I can see clearly how dirty you are," I said.

THIS MORNING WAS IN BLACK AND WHITE

This morning was in black and white,
for the night used up
all the color in the world
for the resplendent dreams
of all the world's brand new lovers.

THIS MORNING WAS AN ECHO

This morning was an echo.
It was not mine.
How could it have been?
I had not spoken.

THIS MORNING WAS STALKING ME

This morning was stalking me.
"O, I thought you were
someone else," the morning said.

THIS MORNING WAS THE ANGEL OF DEATH

This morning was the Angel of Death.
It was not mine.
It was a red-tailed hawk.
It was the angel of the field mouse's death.
The field mouse did not complain.
If my Angel of Death is a red-tailed hawk,
I, too, will not complain.

THIS MORNING SANG

This morning sang.
It sang a wordless song.
It was the song of the oscines.
It was the Dawn Chorus.
I had slept well.
I had slept through the night.
I had slept without awakening.
I celebrated.
I joined the Dawn Chorus.
I was the soloist.
I was the only one who sang the words between the lines.

THIS MORNING HAD A HEAVY HEAD

This morning had a heavy head.
It had a very heavy head.
It lay down next to me.
Its eyes were watery and heavy and gray.
They were very watery and very heavy and gray.
It begged for my light hand on its head.
It begged for my blessing.
Of all the hands, it begged for mine.
Of all the blessings, mine.

THIS MORNING CAME IN ITS SUNDAY BEST

This morning came in its Sunday best.
"Where are you off to?" I asked.
"It's Sunday. I'm going to church," the morning said.
"You filthy liar," I said.
"But many people believe me," said the morning.
"That's not my problem," I said.
"No, it's mine," said the morning.

THIS MORNING *NOTHING*

This morning *Nothing*
took its rightful place
in my life between
Was and *Will Be*.

THIS MORNING I HEARD THE WIND

This morning I heard the wind.
No, it was not the wind.
What I heard were wings.
They were the wings of *Why?*

THIS MORNING WAS NAKED

This morning was naked.
I saw its skin.
Its skin was translucent.
I saw its bones.
Its bones were white.
Its bones were white and heavy and ready
to fall to the earth that was there to welcome them.

THIS MORNING WHISPERED IN MY EAR

This morning whispered in my ear.
"Solonche, you narcissist,
I'm sick and tired of your games," it said.
"So, you've finally learned my name," I said.

THIS MORNING WAS A MIRROR

This morning was a mirror.
"Who is this?" asked the morning.
"I do not know," I said.
"But you knew when it was the night
 who asked," said the morning.
"Yes, but the night asked more lovingly
 than you ask," I said.

THIS MORNING WEPT

This morning wept.
I did not ask why.
I did not try to comfort it.
I knew why.
For that I knew no comfort.

THIS MORNING THE WORLD WAS A DEAD MOON

This morning the world was a dead moon,
for all the dreams that flew up
to the all the moons
from all the nights fell
back to all the worlds as snow.

THIS MORNING WAS A GOLDEN CUP

This morning was a golden cup.
I drank.
I drank all the way down
to the dregs of dawn.
I drowned
the dream that wanted
to keep the dark up
all around me.

THIS MORNING SAID IT WAS SORRY

This morning said it was sorry.
"Do you apologize for lying
  in the dream you sent in the night?"
I asked this morning.
"No, I apologize for telling the truth
  in the dream I sent in the night," said this morning.

THIS MORNING SPOKE GERMAN

This morning spoke German.
I shut my ears.
Even *Die Sonette an*
Orpheus makes me sick to hear.

THIS MORNING WAS A STORM OF LIGHT

This morning was a storm of light.
After I rubbed thunder from my eyes,
I jumped to my feet
and rushed to the window
to survey the damage the storm
had done to the world that it had aged by a single night.

THIS MORNING WAS A BIRD

This morning was a bird.
It was white and black,
both the white and the black were bright,
with a head of red brighter
than the black or the white,
and the head nodded up and down,
agreeing with everything I said.

THIS MORNING TREES DIED

This morning trees died.
I do not know which trees died
or how many trees died,
but I know that trees died in the woods
this morning.
I know because I heard the wind moan in the woods.

THIS MORNING TOOK ITS TIME

This morning took its time.
It knew what I was dreaming.
It wanted me to take my time dreaming it.
It knew I was dreaming of that woman I saw.
The woman in the pharmacy.
The woman I said hello to.
The woman who said hello back to me.
The woman who looked like Dawn Davis.
The woman on whose sofa I passed out.
The woman in whose brownstone I wept my 25 years of tears.
This morning pitied me.
This morning tortured me with pity.
This morning took its time.

THIS MORNING I DID NOT EXIST

This morning I did not exist.
I disappeared sometime during the night.
It was a full moon, yet I disappeared.
It was a full moon and a clear sky, yet I disappeared.
It was a full moon and a clear sky, yet I couldn't be found.
The alarm was raised.
They searched everywhere they could think of,
yet they could not find me.
But they did not search everywhere.
I was where they could not think of.
I was where the full moon told me to go.

THIS MORNING HAD A SECRET

This morning had a secret.
"I will tell you my secret, if you tell me yours,"
the morning said to me.
"You already know all my secrets,"
I said to the morning.
"That is too bad, for now you will never know my secret,"
the morning said to me.

THIS MORNING OPENED MY EYES

This morning opened my eyes.
There was nothing new to see,
so I closed my eyes.
"Ah, now I see," I said to the morning.
"You opened my eyes to the sameness of the world."

THIS MORNING I WAS A STRANGER TO MYSELF

This morning I was a stranger to myself.
I saw the stranger of myself sitting at my desk.
I was not a stranger to the stranger at my desk.
He knew who I was.
He knew I was the stranger of himself sitting at his desk.
And there was nothing strange about it, for he was expecting me.

THIS MORNING I WASTED MY LIFE

This morning I wasted my life.
I wasted it every chance I got.
I wasted it so many times I got very good at it.
I can waste my life at a moment's notice.
I've wasted it hundreds of times.
It is my life.
It is how I live.
It is my daily bread.

THIS MORNING CAME THREE TIMES

This morning came three times.
I wanted nothing to do with the first morning.
I wanted nothing to do with the second morning.
I wanted nothing to do with the third morning.
"You ignored First Morning Sister," said Third Morning Sister.
"You ignored Second Morning Sister," said Third Morning Sister.
"You will not ignore me," said Third Morning Sister.
Then Third Morning Sister took me by the hand and led
    me out into the day.

PART III

ELEVEN MINUTES

For eleven minutes she spoke.
There were enough words to fill eleven minutes.
There was enough memory to fill each word.
It took eleven minutes for her to say what she needed to say.
There was enough memory to make enough words.
Of the eleven minutes, we understood one minute.
Of the eleven minutes, we understood less than one minute.
Of the eleven minutes, less than one minute was ours.
All the rest were hers and hers alone.
For eleven minutes she had a voice.
For eleven minutes she visited us.
For less than one minute she was with us.
She will be back.
She will visit us again.
We don't know when.
It will be unannounced.

ROSES

I was leaving.
I pointed to the wilting roses.

They were in a white vase.
They were whatever was left of red.

"These have seen better days," I said.
"That's the point," she said.

"Yes. It's what love looks like after first bloom, isn't it?" I said.
"Yes, but only if it's the same love in the same vase," she said.

A PARABLE

Fresh, new, beautiful red roses
were happy in their vase, and
the vase was happy with its fresh,
new, beautiful red roses. After
a while, though, the roses began
to wilt and wither, and they wilted
and withered, wilted and withered
more and more, and this made
the vase very, very unhappy, for
there was no room for any more
new, fresh, beautiful roses, be
they yellow or pink or white or red.

DECEMBER PASTORAL

The trees are talking.
"What are leaves?" an oak asks of a birch.

The trees are talking.
"The wind can't hear us," an ash shouts to a sycamore.

The trees are talking.
"It doesn't care, anyway," the sycamore laughs.

The trees are talking.
"Is that we look like naked?" a pine asks a hemlock.

The trees are talking.
"Be quiet. We are never naked," scolds the hemlock.

The trees are talking.
"Look at my crow," says the maple.

The trees are talking.
"Look at my hawk," says the beech.

The trees are talking.
"Look at my moon," says the elm.

OF LOVE

We were in a narrow hallway and could not pass.
She had light blonde hair.
She had light blue eyes.
She had light red lips.
We must kiss, I said.
Why must we kiss? she said.
So that we may be together, I said.
And what shall we do after we kiss? she said.
I had no answer.
You have no answer, and that is why we must not kiss, she said.
She shed a tear, just one.
I shed a tear, just one.
But this was a dream.
And I knew I would awaken.
And this is why I needed no answer.
And this is why we passed in the narrow hallway.
And this is why she shed one tear only.
And this is why I shed one.
And this is why she had a book.
And this is why her name was Deirdre Herrick.
And this was sixty years ago.
And this was sixty years of regret.
And this was sixty years of love.
No, sixty-one years.
Sixty-one years of regret.
Sixty-one years of—O yes, you heard me right!—of love.

A READING

The poet read a poem
in which he said a prayer
to the god of the sun
in the morning and said
the same prayer in the evening
to the god of the moon
and was I surprised to hear
that it was not to the goddess
of the moon that he said
the same prayer to but instead
to the god of the moon because
every poet should know better
than that so I was going to go
up afterward to ask him
about that but I didn't want
to get into a fight with him
and besides what's there to say
to a guy who so clearly can't
tell balls from breasts?

A QUESTION

To the north are mountains.
These mountains are covered in ice.
This ice is smooth as glass, slick as a mirror.
These mountains have edges sharper than razors.
It is impossible to cross these mountains.

To the east are oceans.
These oceans are wider than the earth.
They are deeper than wide.
These oceans are forever boiling.
It is impossible to cross these oceans.

To the south is jungle.
This jungle is darker than the darkest night.
This jungle crawls with bad dreams and worse.
It is impossible to cross this jungle.

To the west is a desert.
On this desert the sun never sets.
This desert is hotter than any furnace.
It is emptier than any emptiness.
It is impossible to cross this desert.

Here is my question.
How did you get here?

NEWS

It is yesterday.
It might be today.
For sure, it is tomorrow.

LIGHT

There was no light at the end,
but there was enough at the beginning
to allow the first step into the dark.

PRIESTESS

She does not look
like one, not the one
I see when I say "Priestess."
She looks like my wife
when she was young, but
O isn't this precisely why
she is the real thing?

NOISE

So delicately balanced,
even the sound of gentle rain
makes my mood come crashing
down around my ears.

STRINGS ATTACHED

Violin. Viola.
'Cello, Double-bass.
They didn't have
to look like women,
did they? O yes they did.
Of course, they did!

NOW AND THEN

I knew what it was
when it was now,
but since it became
then, I have forgotten.

ROSE QUARTZ

Not a living thing,
yet you grow as
though a living thing.
O how I envy you
your crystalline song,
deathless rose.

HORSES

They look sad,
but they are not.
Yet they make
me sad because
they look sad.
It's the fence.

GUARDIAN ANGEL

I need a guardian angel.
I never had one.
I never needed one.
I was always able to be my own guardian.
But I am old, and my reflexes are not sharp anymore.
My eyes are weak.
My peripheral vision is poor.
My ears have lost the higher registers.
So I need a guardian angel.
One with nothing better to do.
One with time on her hands.
One, after all the centuries of showing pity,
with just a little more to spare for me.

THE UNIVERSE

If the universe goes
on forever, then these
words—which I call
a poem—will go on
forever, too. Do not
misunderstand. This is
not a cause for celebration.

"ORANGE BUDS BY MAIL FROM FLORIDA" BY WHITMAN

Do you know "Orange Buds by Mail from Florida" by Whitman?
Do you know it?
If you do not know it, you should find it and know it.
You should go to your library
and find "Orange Buds by Mail from Florida"
or find it in your own dusty Whitman
on your own dusty shelf as I found it in my own
dusty Whitman on my own dusty shelf.
It is a poem that brags about America.
You will laugh when you read it.
You will laugh out loud when you read how Whitman
brags about America in "Orange Buds by Mail from Florida,"
a good clean laugh, without sarcasm, without superiority,
without condescension, a good, clean, wholesome,
American, optimistic laugh.

THE LAKE

The water is low, so
low rocks and
the branches of trees
are exposed. Crows
strut where the swans
once swam.

JUPITER

I was up early.
It was still dark.
As I passed the window, I saw Jupiter.
It was bright.
It was very bright.
It was brighter than any other light in the sky.
It was so bright I forgot everything.
I forgot I was at the window.
I forgot I was an old man going to the bathroom.
I forgot what I learned in school about the solar system.
I forgot what I learned about mythology.
I forgot everything except the word, *Jupiter*,
the name of the light brighter than any other light in the sky.
Then I remembered I was an old man going to the bathroom.

URIEL

Just in case you're wondering,
I'm still here at the garden gate
keeping curious eyes from peering
in, keeping all the wretched out
with my showy sword of fire,
which gets dimmer by the century.
It's not so easy, standing here
like this. I'm really getting weary.
I'm an angel, you know, an angel
and don't have the patience of a saint.
I didn't ask for this lonely hell
of a job. I'd rather fall with Satan
and the rest of his long fallen host
than stay to be the only ever angel's ghost.

MAN GHAZAL

Old English *man(n)*, (plural) *menn* (noun), *mannian* (verb),
    of Germanic origin;
related to Dutch *man*, German *Mann*, and Sanskrit *manu*
    'humankind.'

In Greek mythology, Prometheus shaped from mud the first man.
The Maori believed that the god Tumatauenga created the first man.

In the mythology of the Navajo of North America, Altsé hastiin
    was the First Man.
Mark Twain: "The dog is a gentleman; I hope to go to his
    heaven not man's."

Arthur Schopenhauer: "A sense of humour is the only divine
    quality of man."
Alexander Pope: "The proper study of mankind is man."

Everyone knows H. G. Wells' classic novel (1897) *The Invisible Man*.
Not many people know Ralph Ellison's classic novel (1952)
    Invisible Man.

Almost no one knows Saul Bellow's novel (1944) *Dangling Man*.
Many songs have "man" in the title, but the best is Dylan's
    "Mr. Tambourine Man."

So, Solonche, what more do you have to say, my man?
Only that I want it to be said that he was a real mensch.

MORNING GHAZAL

From the Middle English word "morwening," related to
    German "Morgen" and Dutch "morgen."
In Greek mythology, Phosphorus is the star of morning.

The Romans said Lucifer was the star of morning.
A *pourquoi* tale from Mexico is "Why Rooster Crows
    in the Morning."

Umberto Eco: "I love the smell of book ink in the morning."
Lt. Colonel Bill Kilgore (*Apocalypse Now*): "I love the smell of
    napalm in the morning."

A critically acclaimed movie with Albert Finney (1960) is
    Saturday Night and Sunday Morning.
A B-movie with Robert Stack and Virginia Mayo (1956) is
    Great Day in the Morning.

A song by Aretha Franklin (1964) is "Nobody Knows the Way I
    Feel This Morning."
A song by Irving Berlin (1946) is "I Got the Sun in the Morning."

A man can live five years longer if he kisses his wife every morning.
Most people don't smile before 11:16 in the morning.

    So, Solonche, how are you feeling this morning?
    Not so hot. My doctor said to take two aspirins and call him
        in the morning.

BRAIN GHAZAL

From Middle English *brayn*, from Old English *bræġn*, from
Proto-West Germanic *bragnq*,
from Proto-Germanic *bragną*, from Proto-Indo-European
mreg^{h}nom.

Aristotle thought keeping the heart from overheating was
the function of the brain.
The Egyptians thought it was useless so tugged out through
the nose the brain.

Enough electricity to power a small LED lightbulb (23 watts) is
created by the human brain.
The leech, which is comprised of 32 segments, has 32 brains.

The sperm whale has the world's heaviest (7.8 kg) brain.
The ragworm has the world's smallest (width of a human hair)
brain.

A comedy (2017) directed by Whitney Cummings is *The Female Brain*.
One of the worst films ever made (1968) is *They Saved Hitler's Brain*.

Arthur Rimbaud: "Morality is the weakness of the brain."
Mike Tyson: "I try to catch them right on the tip of his nose
to punch the bone into the brain."

So, Solonche, may we continue picking your brain?
Careful, I'm a poet, you know; you'll find a moonflaw in
my brain.

BOOK GHAZAL

From Middle English *bok, book,* from Old English *bōc,*
from Proto-West Germanic *bōk,* from Proto-Germanic *bōks.*

Most historians agree that the Egyptians invented the
(scrolled) book.
It was the Chinese who invented block printing for a book.

Teeny Ted from Turnip Town (2007) is the world's smallest
reproduction of a printed book.
At 21,450 pages, a conceptual art project based on a Japanese
comic is the world's longest book.

The Bible is the world's best seller, but the second is Chairman
Mao's Little Red Book.
Ernest Hemingway: "There is no friend as loyal as a book."

Jorge Luis Borges: "I cannot sleep unless I am surrounded by
books."
Italian Proverb: "There's no worse thief than a bad book."

A classic Danish silent film (1921) is *Leaves from Satan's Book.*
The 2018 Academy Award winner for Best Picture is *Green Book.*

So, Solonche, haven't you cooked the books?
Absolutely not. I do everything strictly by the book.

ANGEL GHAZAL

Old English *engel*, ultimately via ecclesiastical Latin from
    Greek *angelos*
'messenger'; superseded in Middle English by forms from
    Old French *angele.*

In the Old Testament, the Nephilim were hybrids of humans
    and angels.
In Buddhism and Hinduism, the devas or celestial beings are
    analogous to angels.

In Norse mythology, the Valkyries are analogous to angels.
Thomas Carlyle: "Music is well said to be the speech of angels."

Victor Hugo: "It is by suffering that human beings become angels."
Allen Ginsberg: "Poets are Damned . . . but See with the Eyes
    of Angels."

A comedy (1955) with Aldo Ray and Humphrey Bogart is
    We're No Angels.
Robert DeNiro and Sean Penn star in the stupid remake (1989)
    of *We're No Angels.*

The only hit song (1954) by the doo-wop group The Penguins
    is "Earth Angel."
A classic American novel (1929) by Thomas Wolfe is
    Look Homeward, Angel.

    So, Solonche, are you on the side of the angels?
    Yes, but only if they are the fallen angels.

BLIND GHAZAL

From Middle Dutch *blint*, from Old Dutch *blint*,
from Proto-West Germanic *blind*, from Proto-Germanic *blindaz*.

In Greek mythology, Tiresias, the prophet of Apollo, was,
of course, blind.
The Norse god Hod, son of Odin and Frigg, was blind.

Themis, the Greek goddess of justice, is blindfolded but not blind.
We know about Homer and Milton, but did you know Borges
was blind?

Due to poverty and disease associated with malnutrition,
many early blues singers were blind.
Erik Weihenmayer is the first person to reach the summit of
Mt. Everest who is blind.

Albert Einstein: "Science without religion is lame, religion
without science is blind."
Albert Camus: "The truth, as the light, makes blind."

"White blindness" is the theme of Nobel Prize winner Jose
Saramago's novel (1995) *Blind*.
A song by the great Etta James in her album *Tell Mama* (1968)
is "I'd Rather Go Blind."

So, Solonche, if you had to choose, would you rather be
deaf or blind?
No fair. I'd rather be dumb than either deaf or blind.

DEAF GHAZAL

From Middle English *deef*, from Old English *dēaf*, from Proto-
   West Germanic *daub*,
from Proto-Germanic *daubaz*, from Proto-Indo-European d^hewb^h.

Harpocrates, the god of silence in the Hellenistic religion, was deaf.
In Norse mythology, Vidar, god of vengeance, silence and
   resilience, is deaf.

The popular Japanese god, Ebisu, can be worshiped anywhere
   because he is deaf.
The Roman painter Quintus Pedius was the first person in
   history known by name to be deaf.

Elias Canetti: "Success listens only to applause. To all else it is deaf."
Evelyn Glennie: "I'm not a deaf musician. I'm a musician who
   happens to be deaf."

Jeremih: "Would I have signed to Def Jam if I knew they was
   deaf? Nah."
A horror film (1975), the first feature done completely in
   American Sign Language is *Deafula*.

Sound of Metal is an Academy Award nominated film (2019)
   about a drummer who goes deaf.
A stoner rock album (2002) by the group Queens of the Stone Age
   is *Songs for the Deaf*.

So, Solonche, if you had to choose, would you rather be
   blind or deaf?
Still not fair. I'd still rather be dumb than either blind or deaf.

BREAD GHAZAL

From Middle English *bred, breed*, from Old English *brēad*,
from Proto-West Germanic *braud*.

In about 6000 BC, the Egyptians discovered sourdough bread.
But beer was discovered and brewed long before bread.

The Hebrew slaves left in a hurry, so they took only
    unleavened bread.
During the Thesmophoria festival of Demeter in Eleusis,
    the Greeks left large loaves of bread.

In Norse mythology, Sif is worshiped as a goddess of the
    harvest and of bread.
Miguel de Cervantes Saavedra: "All sorrows are less with bread."

Pablo Neruda: "Peace goes into the making of a poem as flour
    goes into the making of bread."
Scottish Proverb: "Bannocks are better than nae bread."

A comedic short parody (1990) of *Night of the Living Dead* is
    Night of the Living Bread.
In 1921, the Taggart Baking Co. of Indianapolis, Indiana,
    introduced (Ready?) Wonder Bread.

So, Solonche, have you earned your daily bread?
I don't know, for only now have I upon the waters cast my bread.

VIOLIN GHAZAL

"Tenor violin," 1797, from Italian *viola,* from Old Provençal *viola,*
from Medieval Latin *vitula* "stringed instrument," perhaps
from Vitula.

Cremona, Italy, is considered the home and origin of the violin.
Mozart's father, Leopold, in his book about violin playing
referred to the violin as a *fiddle.*

Chen Lianzhi of China created an instrument impossible to
play—the world's smallest violin.
At 14 feet long, a German instrument holds the record for the
world's largest violin.

You can burn 170 calories per hour playing the violin.
There are 150 to 200 strands of unbleached Mongolian horsehair
in the typical violin bow.

Balzac: "The majority of husbands remind me of an orangutan
trying to play the violin."
G. K. Chesterton: "Music with dinner is an insult both to the
cook and the violinist."

The film (1998) that won the Academy Award for best score is
The Red Violin.
In the film *The Devil's Violinist* (2013), actor David Garret
actually played the violin.

So, Solonche, are you feeling as fit as a fiddle?
I am just as long as I'm not playing second fiddle.

HOPE GHAZAL

From late Old English *hopa* (noun), *hopian* (verb), of Germanic origin;
related to Dutch *hoop* (noun), *hopen* (verb), and German *hoffen*.

Elpis was the ancient Greek goddess of hope.
The last goddess was anticipation, the daughter of hope.

In Norse mythology, Lofn is "The Comforter," the giver of hope.
Martin Luther: "Everything that is done in the world is done
    by hope."

Aristotle: "Youth is easily deceived because it is quick to hope."
A historical novel (1993) by Herman Wouk is *The Hope*.

The last track on Pink Floyd's album (1994) *The Division Bell* is
    "High Hopes."
James Earl Jones and Jane Alexander starred in the film (1970)
    The Great White Hope.

A Grand Prix winner at Cannes (1952, shared with *Othello*) is
    Due soldi di speranza.
There are 26 places in America named "Hope" and 13 named
    "New Hope."

So, Solonche, do you still have hope?
Nope, I've given up all hope.

WORK GHAZAL

From Middle English *werken* and *worchen*, from Old English *wyrċan*
and *wircan* (Mercian), from Proto-Germanic *wurkijaną*.

The Hindu goddess Lakshmi represents wealth as long as it is
    gained through hard work.
Ponos was the ancient Greek personification of extreme labor
    and toil, not just hard work.

Edison: "We often miss opportunity because it's dressed in
    overalls and looks like work."
Plato: "The beginning is the most important part of the work."

Aristotle: "Pleasure in the job puts perfection in the work."
John F. Kennedy: "The pay is good and I can walk to work."

A fairly funny Woody Allen movie (2009) starring Larry David
    is *Whatever Works*.
An American pre-Code comedy (1934) with Jack Oakey is
    Shoot the Works.

A suite in D major by Handel (1749) for King George II is *Music
    for the Royal Fireworks*.
A hit song by Rihanna (2016) that contains the word *work* 79
    times is "Work."

So, Solonche, do you think you've done enough donkey work?
Don't know about that, but I'm ready to throw a monkey
    wrench into the works.

SCHOOL GHAZAL

Old English *scōl, scolu*, via Latin from Greek *skholē*,
reinforced in Middle English by Old French *escole*.

The Xia dynasty in China (2070 BC-1600 BCE) created the first schools.
The King's School, Canterbury (597 CE) is Western Europe's
    oldest (and still existing!) school.

In the United States, Boston Latin School (1635) is the oldest
    (and still existing!) school.
Not until the age of seven do kids in Finland start school.

Mealtime is considered part of the curriculum in French schools.
Einstein: "Education is what remains after one has forgotten
    what one has learned in school."

The earliest known preschool series on TV (NBC, 1952) is
    Ding Dong School.
A classic comedy film (1986) with Rodney Dangerfield is
    Back to School.

A song by Tammy Wynette in *Stand by Your Man* (1969) is
    "Don't Make Me Go to School."
A song on the Beach Boys album *Little Deuce Coupe* (1964) is
    "All Dressed Up for School."

So, Solonche, what was your favorite subject in school?
Sorry, I never tell tales out of school.

JEFF AND I TALKED ABOUT THE SUN

Jeff and I talked about the sun
because it finally came out after
two weeks of gray skies and worse,
then about the spring because it
comes earlier every year, then about
the forsythia along my road because
it's all the proof I need that spring
comes earlier, then about our coming
heat death because that's how we
will all die eventually, then about
how Jeff said it won't be the heat but
the humidity because I fed him
the line, then about beer because
the sun finally came out after two
weeks of gray skies and worse, then
about beer tomorrow because it
will be warmer tomorrow than today,
then because the beer will be colder
tomorrow than today, then because his
wife fainted during her chemo yesterday.

DEMENTIA

"Such beautiful skin," she said.

"Such soft and beautiful skin," she said.

"What skin lotion do you use?" the visiting nurse said.

"Baby lotion," the caregiver said.

"Oh baby lotion, of course," the visiting nurse said.

"Of course," I said.

THE TWO CARDINALS

were two brush fires,
the second lit to break
the first, which worked, for
they fought each other off the feeder.

DEMENTIA

From the door,
the only life is her right hand,
the fingers still moving hours after
the *Goldberg Variations*.

THE CONDITION

The acupuncturist asked me
to fill out my medical history.
I listed all the usual conditions,
the same ones I always list—
osteoarthritis, high cholesterol,
sciatica, deviated septum. Then
it asked about something I had
never seen before—*Excessive
dreaming.* What's this? I said.
What is it? she said. Excessive
dreaming, I said. Oh, that means
if you dream too much, she said.
Well, I'm a poet, I said. Oh, then
answer *Yes*, you suffer from excessive
dreaming, she said. Yes, I said. *Yes.*

HOSPITAL

It's a mountain,
this building, the biggest
in this small city where I come
today to take my neighbor home,
this mountain where when my turn
comes, I will come to climb to die.

FAILURE

Poor Schubert.
Poor Franz.
Poor, poor genius.
He so much wanted to be
an opera composer.

I'VE ALWAYS WANTED TO WRITE

I've always wanted to write
a poem on a wall, on
the wall of city hall, or on
the wall of my old high school, or
on the last wall still standing of
a bombed out city, but mostly on
the wall of a temple, as Su Tung-p'o
did when he wrote his poem, "Written on
the Wall at West Forest Temple" in 1084.

I HAVE CHANGED MY MIND

I have changed my mind
about Billy Collins. Not
the poet Billy Collins.
I still don't care very much
for him. No, I've changed
my mind about Billy "Bully-
Boy" Collins, the boss of
the Irish gang that called me
"Four eyes" in school and
followed me in the hallways,
punching me in the back,
exclaiming, "Hey, Four eyes
can take it!" He was right.
I could take it. I still can.

BACH

Thank goodness
he was not a poet.

That's really all
there is to say about it.

WHEN I AM DEAF

When I am deaf and unable to speak,
when I am ready to die
and so unable to go on,
wheel me out into noon's full light
that I may stare up into the sun
long enough to go blind
and thereby give back my eyes
to whatever god it was who created sight.

ABOUT THE AUTHOR

Nominated for the National Book Award, the Eric Hoffer Book Award, and nominated three times for the Pulitzer Prize, J. R. Solonche is the author of 38 books of poetry and coauthor of another. He lives in the Hudson Valley.

SHANTI ARTS

NATURE • ART • SPIRIT

Please visit us online
to browse our entire book catalog,
including poetry collections and fiction,
books on travel, nature, healing, art,
photography, and more.

Also take a look at our highly regarded art
and literary journal, *Still Point Arts Quarterly*,
which may be downloaded for free.

www.shantiarts.com

www.ingramcontent.com/pod-product-compliance
Lightning Source LLC
Chambersburg PA
CBHW072146090426
42739CB00013B/3298